RENDER

RENDER

poems by

Joseph Zaccardi

Poetic Matrix Press

Kate Peper - cover art and design, copyright © Kate Peper.
www.Peperprojects.com

Poetic Matrix Press
P.O. Box 1223
Madera, CA 93639
www.poeticmatrix.com

Dedication

For Jane Kenyon and Su Tung-Po.

They lived on the rays of the sun.

Acknowledgments

Many thanks to the poets, readers, cajolers, and angels who made this book possible; to Anonymous, Calvin Ahlgren, Duff Axsom, Serena Bardell, Rose Black, Richard Brown, James and Joyce Downs, CB Follett, Mary Golding, Karen Hagelund, Karla Clark, Catharine Clark-Sayles, Maureen Johnson, Stephanie Mendel, Kate Peper, John Peterson, Daniel Polikoff, David St. John, Gini Savage, Sandy Scull, Phyllis Tepletz, Susan Terris, Sim Warkov and Al Young.

Thanks to where these pieces were published:
Cam Ranh: Iodine Review of Poetry; Parallel Verses: An anthology.
There is a River: Parallel Verses: An Anthology.
Mined From Clay-Like Soil Called Blue Earth: Iodine Review of Poetry; Parallel Verses: An Anthology.
Something Saved Something Lost: Runes
Mulberry Leaves and the Apple Garden: Poetic Matrix online letteR; Parallel Verses: An Anthology.
Weightless: Parallel Verses: An Anthology.
A Parable: Parallel Verses: An Anthology.
Come Back: Iodine Review of Poetry.
Ties: Parallel Verses: An Anthology.
Palmerton Zinc: Barnabe Mountain Review.
Carl: Parallel Verses: An Anthology.
Prayer: Parallel Verses: An Anthology.
Visiting: Marin Poetry Center Anthology: 2001
Tea Ceremony: Poetic Matrix online letteR.
On the Way from One Place to Another: Southern Poetry Review.

Content

Introduction

The Love comes through

*level of contemplation...depth...tender...connection...
serious...touch...dignified...compassion...arms wide...
horizon...dig into earth...reach sky...hands into the soil
of the world...buddhist sensibility...the love comes through.*

These words have connotations for each of us in our daily life. In this instance, the common thread is the poetic writing of Joseph Zaccardi. I was introduced to Mr. Zaccardi through three exquisite poems he submitted to *Poetic Matrix Press* and its *online periodic lettR* (see online lettR 2 in the *Poetic Matrix* archives) and placed in this volume. "Tea Ceremony," "Search" and "Mulberry Leaves and the Apple Garden" implied to me a depth of understanding of Chinese poetry and sure enough, Joe has extensive study and translation in this area. His poetry excited me, exactly because I had no experience with this area of poetry.

Later I had the chance to meet Mr. Zaccardi at a poetry conference in Berkeley, California and was pleased to find that he is just as kind a person as his writing implies. And now he is my friend.

Hereafter, you will find Joseph's second volume of poetry, <u>Render</u>. I was proud to champion his work to my publisher, John Peterson. John saw the same thing I did in Joseph's work, a deep sensibility and compassion for life. So here is his volume. As you read into the volume, I hope you sense the filaments stretched deep into our world and beyond. And maybe they will reach into you and you will also feel the words. I am honored that Joseph Zaccardi is a fellow poet and friend. Maybe he will become your friend, too. And then you will feel the love come through.

—James Downs, Yosemite poet

RENDER

It is better to sink into the deepest
part of the Nine Pools
than to live among dishonest men

He who sinks in the Nine Pools
should prepare to swim
He who sinks among dishonest men

can have no hope

– Confucius

Tr. by DiCarza

SECTION I:

LESSENS

Every stream on every mountain stops
when it enters a lake.

—Han Shan

There is a River

There is a river near Hue called Perfume;
its water is red, amber during the monsoons.
There is a factory that processes rubber,
trees with thick green leaves, barks bleeding white.
Birds come from around the world to drink
from the river. I used to watch them hop, dip
their heads, then leap up into air, folding
their legs back like a jet's wheels, like Corsairs.
And there is someone named Du Thanh Mai
who once took me into her house, fed me
rice with her fingers, while I tilted my head
back and chewed. She showed me her white
jade Buddhas. And said, I should listen
to the stars out in her small garden because
they could sing. There was a cot to lie upon,
around us bamboo and boxes of lilies, some burnt
orange, some white, some darker. And one
that was green with white pistils.
There was fragrance and river sound. I know
we both cried, and if either of us slept,
it was pretend.

For a Long time

For a long time I couldn't touch the scars.
Nightmares came in colors. I would turn
seventeen times an hour, hear each minute
passing. What eats at the flesh eats at the soul.
For a long time I couldn't touch anyone, couldn't
shake hands without wanting to pull away.
My kisses were hard, drew blood from
the well of others. Now I'm in the fading zone,
gray on gray. What I hear at night is echo,
lost voices. Where I can touch, is now dulled.
In my sleep nothing comes, and the days
move slowly as if searching.

Cam Ranh

Vietnam 1970

Out on the tin roof of a barracks. It is dark
and the heat blankets my naked body.
My eyes blur the lightness. Stars
look exhausted. The sound of locusts,
sharp, brilliant. A green fragrance
I can't put into words. And I am so small.
Everywhere there are rivers and mountains.

California 2005

I am writing in another place, in another time,
an ocean apart, carved slabs with the marks
of days, years on a hinge.
I squeeze my pen wanting more to come
but by now I hear street sweepers making
their rounds, the clearing, so that moment
on a roof has slipped to the insignificant.
I can remember some beauty in the rotten
war and know I'm adrift, not done writing
when it comes to me. It rained. I kept
my eyes closed and laughed, stayed
there, let the water have me.
How could I have forgotten?

Something Saved Something Lost

As far as tales go, here's one with trouble in it,
and a little history, like the alleys I used to haunt
looking for something – how I cried one time
in an offbeat bar in a Japanese port-of-call,
openly, so that one of the girls hustling drinks
from customers, came and sat by me, held me,
waited till I could talk, till sounds came smoothly,
not in jerky gulps. How I bought her a shot of tea
for a thousand yen. She gave me a red aster,
and I hurried back to my ship and put it in the middle
of a book I was reading because "naked" was in the title.
I thought I'd save this flower forever, pressed
as it was between the hard covers and the weight
of what the pages contained, twenty-two chapters,
the same number as my age at the time.
But when I look for it now, in all the boxes
lugged from place to place, it isn't there,
and I have almost come to believe
it never was.

Fumiko

She had the smell of sweet chin chu, could fold
into a crane. Black hair hung down the middle
of her back. We each had wounds. My need
was to touch her; hers was to feel. It was a sunny day,
white birds fluttering in the trees. She wanted to see
2001 A Space Odyssey. I don't remember the year.
Fumiko walked the ten paces behind as required. Inside,
she fell asleep, mumbled words I couldn't understand
during the part of the movie where there's a crystal
monolith. I watched her breathe, watched as the credits
flared on the screen, unfolding. Outside, flying
white birds like scraps of paper.

Regret

What I forget is kept on a long list, white tape
of a cash receipt. It unfurls, accounting for debits,

each detail printed in a blue smear. If I try to recall
the young North Korean woman in Yokosuka,

a refugee who took a revered Japanese name,
I can't. Or the meal she prepared the night before

I shipped out, or our clothes piled on tatami, I can't.
I can't remember nearly missing first call to colors,

or hesitating at the gangway, saluting the ensign,
or almost not leaving.

Thursday

If on this particular day I had not needed the new Neruda translation.
If I'd gone to Book Depot instead of Book Beat. If I'd waited
till after lunch. If you hadn't heard the hurrying inside my chest,
hadn't brushed your hand slightly against mine.
I would've spent the rest of my life that much lessened.
What if you hadn't said anything, and I said nothing?
Our little stealth would've gone unnoticed by the coffee drinkers
and the journal writers. And you would have given me change.
I would have taken change as something to save in a jar.
Just as Neruda could have become a math teacher, adding
to the consequences. There'd be nothing of us.
You see how close we came to missing?

Blues

The week is filled with rain, with breaks
now and then. Blues, coming from a Hi-Fi
blocks away layer the neighborhood
with alto sax. I stand facing west, the wet
coming on strong, the day lessens,
the hour gains. Now someone who likes
trombone turns up the sound.

Illumine

I watch you watch yourself dance in the mirrored wall.
Strobe lights, red and black lights. Why do I love you?
Because you love yourself without mercy for others.
I know you have already turned against me, bored
with my flesh. Two girls writhe in a cage, old men tuck
bills in their G-strings, get to touch. I order another drink,
a double this time, check the mirror behind the bar
through bottles. What is reflection if not desire?
With it comes devastation.

After

After drinks, after dinner at Alfredo's,
we ride to the beach. After the waves pull
away and the winds turn their backs from us,
we make our way to your flat on 43rd. There,
the soundless candles, the curtains faded
at the bottom from the sun's wear.
You put on an album called "Endless".
Love works only as long as it takes,
and the beat inside stops. I am lying
beside you; you are lying beside me.
After, we wait for morning, for the early
sounds of dogs pulling against tethers,
joggers pounding pathways. The curtains
stir; birds clamor. There is movement
and indecision between high and low tide.
The opposite ends.

Break

They pretended to talk.
They walked the old pier, the pilings
encrusted with mussels. The repeating
surf, the harsh cry of gulls feeding.
Each knew what the other wanted. Under
their feet the waves' whitewash. As each one
spoke their voices surprised. Turning around
as the day bled, the sea ebbed. When longing
is lost, lovers hold a breath, to prolong.

Desolation

Fire has blackened, taken all that was alive.
The remains of a fence no longer separate –
wooden posts ash, the chicken wire vaporized.
Wind has taken the shapes away. A toolshed
with a wheelbarrow leaning up against it, an imprint.
Acres of pine, blue sagebrush gone. Wounds
never meld perfectly, they leave rills. When you left
me. When I left you. The earth takes its fill. Old roots,
dormant seeds reawaken. The breaking down
and the building. We thought if we could hold on,
but it's all gone, even the need is gone.

Bullets

He carried two in his right pants' pocket,
.38 caliber, lucky pieces, charms for not buying the farm.
In his left pocket: scraps of paper, a lined out
grocery list, an expired bus transfer, the start of a poem
or maybe the end: "Held her the way a man holds /
a woman when he's in trouble…" He'd roll them
like dice in his palms when he was nervous.
He almost threw them into the outtake of bay water
under the Golden Gate, another time washed them
in his jeans at the laundromat; in the dryer they broke
free, sounded like the knock of a belt buckle, a silver
dollar, but he got them out, burned his fingers
for the effort, slipped them into another pants' pocket
for a change, where they radiated, cooled. They'd rub
together when he walked the promenade at the Presidio,
sleep like warm bodies when he sat on the bench
as he counted the cargo ships coming and going
through the channel. One day, evil music going through
his head, he might push them into their chambers,
cock the gun, pull the trigger. If they were duds
he'd call her, maybe she'd answer or call back.

Mined from Clay-like Soil
Called Blue Earth

I have been studying a lump of amber, the shape
of a human heart, the shape of a horn of plenty.
The bodies of insects stopped forever in whatever
they were doing 30 million years ago. Polina,
who sold me the amber, said it was at least that old,
from the Baltic steppes, from the bleeding resin
of ancient pines. And perhaps it is morbid
to turn them under an incandescent light, to see
their tiny legs and antennae magnify, almost move.
And Polina gave me some czarist-style chocolate, dark
and rich with cocoa butter, to go with my purchase.
For once I didn't mind overpaying, and these insects,
caught as they are, don't seem to mind, if I can speak
for them, their immortality.

Key

I am outside clipping the dead from the roses,
the leaves spotted with rust, and lopping off the dry,
flat heads of yarrow, sending cuttings over the side
of the deck, down the steep slope crowded
with bay trees, tangles of poison oak. The deer
come by now and then to nibble at the sweet
droppings. Sure footed, they pass over the bitter.
I eat a peach, toss the pit where I think it may
have a chance to take root. I am almost religious
in my hopes and disappointments. My fingers,
sticky with the kind of red that comes from under
the skin of this fruit, dig in my pocket for something
to wipe my hands on, and somehow my housekey
comes out, pitches over the railing, gone.
I lick the juice from my fingers, taste the salt
of the flesh, try to remember where I hid
the spare key, laughing aloud at my luck,
laughing at the things I've thrown away.

SECTION II:

PARABLES

*Those who have a stringent code of morals
have a greater respect for the devil.*

–Su Tung-Po

Walking in the Woods Toward Jade Mountain

In the green world there are green birds,
and they hop on the tops of lichee trees
and eat the sweet flesh. You would not know
they were there except for their singing,
but if your ears are stuffed full with your
own thoughts or the music of daydreaming,
they will pepper you with seeds and shake
the green light with their green feathers.
They will perch on branches of green willow,
talk in their green language until you listen.
They know all the stories in every tongue
by heart, and know each word is a gift
having more than one meaning. They know
the Chinese sound for ten thousand
was once the same as the sound for scorpion.
To the green birds, there is no difference.

The Rain and the Water

Feeling change makes my heart ache,
said Li Po, in the Legend of the White Deer.

White deer, who carried immortals
on their journeys between worlds.

I inspect a footbridge, in my own way,
lean over the pilings and measure mentally

how much soil and gravel eroded
after eight inches of rain. Though I know little

of engineering, I do know what holds. The piers
look solid, old cement from the '40s, well seated.

I check the planks by stomping and shaking
the handrail put in last year, already etched

by teenagers who don't know mortality but do
know want, and desire, and who's kissing whom.

What sighs, what washes and salves the streambed?
Wei Sheng, a young man of the Zhou dynasty,

the spring and autumn period, promised to meet
a girl under the Lù Shān Bridge,

continued

but she was late in coming, and as the water rose
he clung to the bridgepost and drowned.

As I think this, a dun-colored doe
comes to the creek and drinks.

From the Lower Path to Higher Ground, Returning

Midday, the summer winds howling
from the coast twenty-five miles away. Hightailing
between hills, tearing at limbs of oak and madrone,
the Indian willows along San Anselmo Creek.
I see the currents undulate. I lean into the flood.
Great redwoods bend and twist. I hear the cries
of women, cries of men. Winds mourn. Hills despair
for the unreachable, while the earth holds the trees
and won't let go.

The sea and wind go beyond understanding.

There are wounds in my heart, and I bear down,
walk the gnarled streambank toward higher ground.
As I rise, the winds die. It is like the sea escaping.
Han Shan says every stream on every mountain stops
when it enters a lake. A doe, eyes filled and empty,
trembling ten feet from me. I stand still.
It is Han Shan. We meditate, listen. Seek not answers
but understanding, he says, to know the self,
one must look into the self. I hold my hand
toward her muzzle; she licks the salt from my palm.
I am calm. Han Shan turns and the she-deer is gone.
The afternoon sun lowers. I walk the few miles
down to the road.

Search

Because of its complaint, I come to the sea.
Because it is placid on the outtake. I come
to understand what can't be understood –
the gravity, the pull of forces. What can be
felt, carries both regret and remorse, a yoke
digging in at the blades of the body. The whole
body. Aimless, pulling along weight. I spread
a blanket on sand, anchor the corners
with driftwood, with the shell of a sea turtle.
Set out bread, pure water. Before this altar,
I wait to be lifted.

Glass House on a Side of a Hill
Overlooking the San Geronimo Valley

Teacher taught: Every sin begins with a lie.
When I was young, I stole crabapples
from Mrs. Halpern's backyard, tore my iridescent
pants on her cyclone fence leaving, and got
stomach cramps after eating the hard fruit
that was both sweet and tart. Until that day,
I hadn't lied. Today, twelve hours before the fall
equinox, the hills hunch under cloudless blue sky.
I stare at the emptiness, silent. He also said something
to me about truth: Every true word is a word you don't have
to remember. And now a blue jay flies down from the blue
spruce to my deck, steps close to the glass wall. She does
not see her sharp eyes in reflection, nor her beauty.
She lives on the outside of where I live. She sees only
a golden striped spider, silent and waiting in a web
at the nexus of beams. Another time, teacher said:
Look into the hearts of things; don't put trust in words only.
The blue jay hops up to the rail, then flies off
toward the hills.

Midori

You lead the way
toward lush ravines,
earth glowing
with rain, air green
with oxygen.
Tightroping on troughs
of water, you dance,
arms outstretched.
You name
the many names of water.
Water carried up
by the weight of air,
water held
on the underleaf of ficus,
runnels on cliffs of lava,
black, iridescent,
water that sings
in shadow, sings in sun,
bridges islands, continents,
seeps into thirsty earth,
slides invisibly
on smooth-tongued rock.
We embrace,
sheer water
flowing over our bodies,

continued

fingers veiling
our faces,
these nets
catching the last
        drops.

Tea Ceremony

The pouring movement mirrors music
on the temple's slope, rain. Unblossomed
cherry trees outside, gemmed. Jasmine: clouds
of locusts, the clearing of things. Bonay: healing.
Mint: cleansing, purification. And in the dregs,
the reading. Images fill, thoughts transform. We lean
forward, listen in trance, feel the warmth of the body,
smell sweetening air with its slow dance
of excitement. It is said when Li Po saw the whole
round moon, he went into the lake, feeling
nothing of the moon – only undertow, the pull
of faraway, the way tea changes water,
the way reflection shimmers reflection.

Two Jade Bowls Empty Except for the Light They Hold

She lives in an old house of frame and grass.
Today she rubs her charm, worries it
between thumb and finger. It is strung
on a gold chain: A carving of a smiling Buddha –
its strength comes from the fine needles
that mesh and interlock. Perfect harmony.
The first piece of jade must be a gift.
This was from her lover. After he left
to fight with the Kuomintang, she purchased
two jade bowls from the ruins of An-Yang.
Held to light they illuminate a rabbit
on a green moon. It has been five decades.
She remembers his voice, his smell.
The pendant slips from her grasp, shatters.
The slivers reflect; the gold chain recoils,
hisses at the cheap fake. Some flaws
are nearly imperceptible. The roof
is made of palm fronds, bamboo rafters,
and lets in some light.

From the Empress Hsi-Ling-Shi

The mulberries will soon bear white fruit.
On thin branches silkworms
feed on heartshaped leaves.
In early summer they will spin their silken
threads, spin silk threads as a gift.
We will take the cocoons, boil them,
and after the throwing, weave fine coats,
embroider them, wear all the colors
of snapdragons, chrysanthemums.
In the court of the Yellow Emperor.
In the court of the Red Emperor.

Mulberry Leaves and the
Apple Garden

When I look, I see deer foraging. They are eating
winter apples. And the leafless trees are heavy
from three weeks of rain. When I look again, I see
deer's breath, their soaked coats. They walk
noiseless, hooves imprinting the giving soil.
In the Sui dynasty, among the three kingdoms,
the Emperor Yangli was known to be the most depraved
and extravagant. He so disliked winter; he ordered
leaves and flowers of silk fastened to the bare palace trees.
In spring, before the first green bud, the emperor died.
His concubines wept; his sixty-seven sons wept.
The silk merchants, the silk spinners counted their coin.
And, it is said, unicorns ate the silk flowers, the fallen leaves.

Second Growth

Mostly manzanita, some madrone.
And set back on the upslope, a cabin
to sleep ten, lofts and ladder.
Near midnight, spring, no one out and about.
I'm in the second growth, after the clearcut
of redwoods, the stumps alive in their decay.
No place to sit. No vacancy.
All trails end at the Eel, beached up
limbs of the weather-worn, the wind-torn.
I'm reading Charles Wright's *Appalachia*.
The Coleman lamp sputters kerosene
fumes; the last line in the book floats up:
The tops of trees know no heights.
But when I look again, it reads:
Until there is nothing else.

Airborne

This is stratus, and this, cumulus and cirrus.
And here the sun, the great solipsist, above
water, on rock face, into the overhill. This
is the wind, the stratosphere, layers of hot
and cold. Fog in commingling. And this
is the waking. The hawk, the eagle, the bee
and gnat, the little and great. And above
all this, the outer, the whole. Heavens idle
in the view. And below is the held down,
the moved, which is worked by the moon.
And the living who repair the cracks
and splinters, who look up and down,
who wait to leave, who want to stay, and
who follow into the lifted, and the nether,
and that which is everything.

Harvest

Every place I've lived, I've put two stones outside the door.
This time, one of agate, from back home, about the size
of a softball, and next to it, from my new backyard, a brittle
shard of claystone, striated with iron, maybe copper.
This is balance, a fair swap of the solid. In the same way
I leave some food on my plate to give back, to make penance.
And when most of my life is gone, I'll lay one stone
with me, listen to its opaque speech, feel the weight —
just as the medieval serfs buried a sacrificed lamb
for the acres sown, and a priest would chant
and write in runes.

Grace

I remember a crash site. In the wake of a gunship
there is quiet, and trees moving are quiet.
Memory, the wreckage of what war leaves,
falling in its darkness. I'm thinking this while cutting
pasillas, scraping out seeds with my thumb.
And I am chopping onions. Oil heats in a skillet,
my eyes burn from the vapors. What can I say
of a world that honors its dead by preserving its ruins.
Now there is the smell of onions caramelizing,
peppers softening. There will be food on the table,
and patches of light from the fading day
coming in through the window, the blending of things –
the food I put in my mouth, the grace I say.

Gathering

Tomorrow, as first light stretches
through untroubled woods, a mist will lift
from decaying leaves along the fire trail.
Wild grapevines will drop gangling shadows
from gray branches of club oak and chestnut oak.
Tomorrow, I'll go to the library at closing time,
in the Borough of Jim Thorpe, to photograph
a glass case of local birds composed
by a Schuylkill taxidermist in 1875.
Attracted to killed beauty, to the perfect,
I'll drive back with the windows down,
past man-high corn. The day after tomorrow
I'll pore over proofs, the one-by-one squares,
pick the best to enlarge.
There's a kindness to death.
To the gathering.

Mount Tam

We hear the call of fog horns as we climb over
fallen leaves. Hold hands on the slippery path

under pines dripping nine-tiered cones.
Mushrooms, red-topped, chanterelles egg-yellow

thrust toward sparse light in bracken and birch.
We rise slowly to a clearing on the ridge.

All this way to picnic and drink wine
that taste of oak and butter.

Wild Mushrooms

Growing on the upslope, where the earth smells wet,
the scent of leaf decay everywhere. I find them.
Always the unexpected. Always overnight magic.
Pushing up through mulch, near rotting wood, they appear.
The forbidden fruit of the dead, resurrection of the unearthly.
And I have this urge to eat them, taste their raw flavor.
As a joke, I once planted store bought portabellas
at the base of an old stump, pretended
to pick them as some friends arrived for brunch.
The look on their faces made me feel cruel.
And the afternoon didn't go well; a level of mistrust pervaded.
Why is it called practical to have knowledge over others
or weakness to be kind? Still, they ate the warmed
mushrooms, thinking perhaps we could be saved by this act.

A Parable

The villagers wrap white stones in the fronds
of areca, put them out in the sun. And the sun
comes and goes, comes and goes. And the gods think
all this is special fish prepared for them. They are pleased.
During spring festival, paper is put in red envelopes
in place of money and set afire. And the moon pushes
and pulls, pushes and pulls. And the gods think
they have been paid. Again the gods are pleased.
When the monsoons don't come, when locusts swarm,
the people blame themselves, not the gods.
They ask the priests to burn more incense, to chant
louder. The people don't know the gods can act
as though they cannot hear, act as though they cannot
speak, anytime they choose.

Parable II

I travel a road.
Neither a steep drop nor a steep rise.

What is it paved with?

Neither gold nor fool's gold.
Neither remorse nor reward.

Where does it take you?

The world is round.
It takes me to the start of the rise, to the end.

Why do you travel this road, not another?

This I cannot answer, but I know
we can neither choose nor refuse.
The world lets us go only when it is ready,
and almost always when we are not ready.

Weightless

A bird plummets to earth. Nothing is weightless forever.
It is a mistake to think there is freedom from gravity,
that rapid beating is perpetual. No heart can do it.
Why does a bird dog seek and find a kill? to please?
One species from another takes. This is a fall
that mocks; this is the gods turning the tables.
It is how they greet us, how they say goodbye.

What is Light

Trapped in a room. One lamp does the trick,
transforms the circular to the ovate, marks
a boundary across the rug, hard-oak floorboards,
travels upward to the cornice, angles one
way toward dark, another toward diffusion.
I lounge in an overstuffed chair, impression
of the self melding, giving in to its easiness.
And outside? The mystery of dark. When light's
gone, there's nowhere for silence to go.
A doorless space without walls, an echo without...

Waterchain

A body will take everything. In the piercing
will be filled, in the fasting will be nourished.
The fonts in the church hold what's holy, water
and tears. The body is the temple.

This is our lesson, the catechism, memorized,
imprinted. At the altar we will all someday lie,
the sacrifice, the Christ. Iron holding body to wood.
This is the judgment, the devouring and emptying.
It is water that holds us, surrounds, captures.

Floating

The water is green.
On the bottom, sharp rocks
silkened with algae.
I float in this beauty.
Each ripple alters, reforms around.
I am a body in the spirit
circling in still foam.
Water a blessing.
And I need to be blessed.
Each fan of my arms anoints,
each kick propels.
I am changed and see and hear
the change. Clouds lean
in the view. I come to the center
of the quarry,
almost panic over the depth,
force myself to calm, steady
my breath, let the subtle undertow
take me in its drift back
to where the sun warms,
to the rest.

Awake

I wake to sounds of the sea
because I have fallen
asleep while sun bathing.
And I think how funny it is
to compare sleep with falling
or to bathe with sun
and watch patches
of sky move. Something sad
is stirring. The surf comes forward.
And someone has made
a teepee from driftwood.
A dog chases and retreats.
I start to sing, as I might
in church, then hum,
as I would when happy
or frightened.

SECTION III:

LESSENS

The knees fail easily when the gods will have it so.

—Giorgios Seferis

Question

What is life? My little brother asks in his faraway voice.
I hold my breath, but all breath escapes. And the waves
divide time. I try to come up with the perfect answer:
each grain of sand on earth carried to heaven
by an angel. Isn't that eternity, he says?

Too much time is spent.

The little sister I can't remember runs into the surf.
I follow. The sound and feel, neither answer nor understanding.
Now my little brother bobs in the water, laughs when a wave slaps
the back of his head.

And in that deep place without memory,
we are held.

Random Recollection

She was maybe thirty-five and I was younger.
One time I saw she had a shiner, a bruiser
that had turned yellow at the edges, like the leaf
on a house plant struggling. She lived
in the apartment next to mine, had a live-in
she called her man-friend, who always had
a long cigar stuck in his mouth, and he would
grunt if anyone said hello. He wore a dark suit
and topcoat no matter what. She rang my bell
saying she had phone trouble and could I
take a look-see. They had a big fight that night,
pots and pans. The manager said she moved out
without notice the next morning. I need to know
if she's still around; why I don't know, and him,
I don't give a rat's ass. And for the record
the phone was shot, is all I know.

From Baker Beach to the Golden Gate

Here the walking is good, the topography giving
under my feet, and miles of wet life overlapping.
A stiff breeze blurs. I top the sand dunes
by taking three steps to gain two, walk between
parked cars that look like graveyard
mausoleums, to the two-lane road. On one side,
the army housing of the Presidio, on the other,
ragged ocean, choppy cliffs. It will take me
an hour to get to the bridge, another fifteen minutes
to reach midspan. Already I can hear the hum
of traffic, the low growl of baywater rushing
under and out. My thoughts wander
to the last time I was here, nine or ten years ago,
making subtle shifts to memory, rewriting
the day colder, inking treelines as stark as pitch
against a gray sky. I am changing things. Pulling
the disparate together: those who leapt, those
who walked away, and the man who wrote
in his suicide letter that he wouldn't jump
if only one person smiled at him.
I reach midpoint, the two towers holding
steel cables, I lean over the rail, sing
to the blue-green gods,
to the quiet below.

Come Back

You can watch the grass grow, as the saying goes,
but not under your feet. There it will not. I'm thinking
of a soldier, a friend, though friend comes first, in the time
of year when it's hot and muggy in Kinderhook, New York,
when if you're patient, and he was (though I wanted
time to slow, to reverse, like H. G. Wells' time machine),
you could see the grass wiggle and get taller. And he says,
at least he won't have to mow this damn acre anymore
(still puffing on "the cigar-eets"). We start singing
a Jim Morrison song: "Show me the way to the next
whiskey bar..." – our alma mater when we were in
the service – until he runs out of breath, and I'm holding
my hand over my mouth so he won't know I'm cracking.
But he thinks it's because I'm tone deaf, having once said
my whistle was two tones of wind, and he says, after
wheezing, he needs to rest and will I come by tomorrow.
By now the grass as high as corn, as impenetrable
as bamboo.

Ties

Over forty years ago:

Two boys walk on ties between rusted rails the old way,
their arms over each other's shoulders.
Queen Anne's lace fills the ditch, careless, ordinary, beautiful.
The boys stop and one presses his ear to the long iron,
he hears the world turning, mourning.
His friend watches the narrowing tracks on their quiet journey.

At the hospital, over forty years later:

You are choking on white air, the invisible,
your lungs filling with liquid and your own breath.
If I could change places, I would. The sky will still be the sky.
If I could, I'd make the sun travel back through its language of time.
If we could run away, make this chapter another,
I would change places, put my ear to the hum, heat of the rail,
listen for your blood, the white part.

Before you die:

My hand is in your hand the way men hold hands.
I think, what have we become, old friend,
and watch not you, but the clock as though I could turn
back to that day, that day we somehow knew
was important, unchangeable, ours no matter what.

continued

Now this sound of air decompressing. In two minutes
I've relived the past we shared; you moving away
like the black speck of a crow disappearing
on the blue fabric.

Something's Wrong

What was it I used to feel? What was it?
In the pup tent where we slept, the clear wet smell of the lake,
the Newport cigarettes we smoked, the way menthol tasted blue
on the back of the tongue. How you wouldn't let me blow out the candle
because you wanted to see what my eyes looked like closed.
You said you'd always be my best friend, even when we grew up,
married – said I should talk to no one, tell no one. I was holding you,
you were holding me, the lake freezing over with pollen when I fell
asleep, the dark between the flash of birch trees, eye flutter. They say
when you OD'd you had the shakes, tracks on your arms and legs.
Your last words: "Something's wrong." A bad batch of horse, you riding
off into the woods. I'll never forget, not any part. Even the part
I could not see, the part I could not feel. I did not look
to see if your eyes were open. I never told anyone.

Palmerton Zinc

I was carrying groceries on the hard
snow-packed street.
The sidewalks were buried somewhere,
and fire hydrants, and maybe
a child's bike left out a little too long
before a storm swept the starkness away,
scrubbed this small Pennsylvania town clean.
Repaved it measure by measure –
by lot, by acre, by grid.
A siren echoed through the abandoned
zinc factory, brushed the ice-tipped birches outside.
Normally I pay little attention to ambulances,
because normally they continue on their way until
the wails are only dogs howling
at the sounds of themselves, but today
it turned the corner almost as I turned the corner
and stopped almost as I stopped
at the mangled red metal sled
wrapped around a boy of ten, so broken
I could only whisper, *oh my God.*
That night I tried to write this down,
tell someone of the unbearable,
but my hand shook, would not work.
Snow kept falling through this black
and damaged night of winter,
kept repaving,
kept me awake with the sound of falling.

A Portrait

There on the mantel you'll see it:
a photo of all of us.
Only now so few remain.
We're there though, claiming immortality.
We pose on the seaside porch.
The second to last step has a warped board
that gives off such a squeak,
everyone comments. It's good, that sound.
It's the kind that doesn't need fixing.
It's tuned perfectly to the wicker furniture
and the old handmade rocker
that's been in the same spot
since pre-depression days.
Two rose-of-Sharon bushes
flank the Queen Anne porch,
and in the gable above is a small window
holding a pot of geraniums.
After our smiles broke away,
we ran down to the beach and watched
a serious horseshoe game. Played tag.
Let the cool sand squish
between our toes.
Past the ringers, and the waves
running sideways on this day,
we were so close to where it all started.
Aching in the warm sand,
we remembered ourselves.

Carl

So now your name is tangible,
part of the title on a marquee.
Your picture on a poster, framed.
As hard as I try I can't parse your face,
the commas won't fit around the eyes,
the brackets of teeth aren't right,
your hair in quotations will not do.
The theater lights dim, the dot
of projection on the back wall widens
to a perfect rectangle on the screen.
Logo of PBS in the center,
the roll of credits: Thanks to the many
foundations, viewers (like us)
and oddly the SHELL Corporation.
A streetcorner game comes to my mind,
a scam of lucre, poker, chance, flimflam.
Like HIV, hiding behind Capitals.
Now you see me…now you don't.
In the darkness, you are the sun,
all revealing. You talk about your body
in the third person, *his* ribs shrunken
to the frame of a pomegranate, *his* waif-like body,
his skin like muslin. Similes touching.
I remember you said you wouldn't
make love in the dark any longer.
What you see is what you get. Always
the master of cliché, the quick retort.
Now look at you, your face
punctuated, memorable.

Forever

He is telling me the story of how a raindrop forms,
how drops fall from the clouds. About the filling
and emptying. We are a speck on the miles of beach
at Sandy Hook. Curling south and north the coast
disappears in a filigree of mist, the stirred up salt.
And the winds licking at strands of sea grass, taking
some of his words away. Washing and washing.

He is telling me this again, with his eyes,
in the urgent care unit, the respirator taking
and giving. I wipe the tearing from the corners
of his eyes, the spittle from the mouth. He holds
my hand, unblinking. His hair sticks to damp skin.
The heart monitor's green line escaping. I ask
him to tell me again about the raindrops, the forming.
His breath coming deeper. He submits
by explaining forever with his breathing,
then not breathing.

Render

He rolls a hardboiled egg between the palms of his hands,
peels away the shell, tosses the white bits on the ground.
Am I the reincarnation, he says. You're chicken shit,
she answers, pass the salt.

This is my body; this is my blood; she swirls the wine, the glass
taking on a coat of burgundy. He sticks his tongue out at her
for the effect, the play on words. They taught each other to make
love: a light repast, wine, and this body giving to that body.
Becoming one.

She remembers love, and more: nails, thorns, long knives.
The bitter soaked in brine for the curing. What takes away, gives.

After the Ascension, Mary Magdalene enters the court of Caesar Tiberius,
complaining how poorly Pilate behaved, and tells him Jesus lives again.
To explain, she picks up an egg from the table. Tiberius responds:
a man can no more rise from the dead than the egg in your hand
can turn red. The egg turns red.

Tennessee Williams said, "It is uncertain that lovers can drive out
demons with the gift of an apple or the twist of an arm." In other words,
it's uncertain if taking sustenance (ask Adam and Eve) improves
the soul, if making love is enough.

The breakdown of an animal is called rendering: food, feed,
fertilizer, soap, lipstick. Nothing is unused.

Jane

After Donald Hall

His wife has died.
He visits each day
for seven days
her grave,
seven years, seventy years, seven hundred years
he ages.
His wife the poet.
He studies pictures taken of her,
her on the beach, floppy hat working the wind,
waves licking at her sand-speckled feet.
Pictures of her at museums, drinking in Vermeers,
at a party laughing, laughing in pictures, eyes wide and brown,
laughing captured, pictures of her bald from chemo
framed on the mantel.
He feels the heat from the hearth,
flushes at a sound like
footsteps. Hers?
No. Alone.
He studies pictures
of his
young wife.

Holding

I look up and over
the slight rise of a hill. Under
a triangle of maples, a picnic
table laden with food: fried
chicken, potato salad, French
bread, baked beans, and in thick
ruby slices, watermelon.
But no one has come, not one yellow jacket
hovers. The ants have sent out
scouts. The queen fidgets
in her lair. Flies follow wrong
currents. I drift toward the redwood
table, circumventing.
Everything's perfect: wine chilling
in a chest, two stemmed glasses
on ice. I touch nothing; this is
my life.

Del Sol

I have visited many times the surfaces
of desolation, many times the deserts.
Walked parched in shadows, lay blistered
under the intense. Squinted in the glare,
tried making water from sand, tried
drinking from the mirage, a fountain
of dust. Why I go to these places, looking
for the hidden, the unseen, is to hear the sound
not heard. The map on the monument
that says "You Are Here" tells me nothing.
My finger turns inward. I step closer, into
blur, mouthing, I am here.

Nothing

What is the world without the world?
So much depends on perspective.
If a straight line is drawn from point "A"
to infinity, it will eventually begin to curve,
so said Einstein. Everything turns
on itself: the earth, our sun, a dog
tied to a Maypole. And who will be sorry
if "nothing" is uncovered, who will care
if there's no world at the end?

Prayer

I've finished with the weeds, scalped them low
to the ground, spared the dandelions, forget-
me-nots, ferns growing around the piers
of my deck. Spent half a day. Had chicken salad
for lunch, now stare at a bowl of ripe peaches,
Fuji apples, think about the fresh corn I'll eat tonight,
the barbecued short ribs. The windows are burnt-out
with light. Everywhere the growing goes on.
By three this afternoon the wind will pick up,
the green trees freshened. I move to chair and table,
put my pen to work – start writing.
If it works out, I'll have a glass of wine, Riesling,
and if it's a good poem, I'll break the glass in the cold
fireplace for luck, to give thanks.

SECTION IV:

LEARNING

And he who makes his law a curse,
By his own law shall surely die.

—William Blake

Runway

I climb over the legs of an aisle passenger
to the window seat, buckle down, look through
the port at those waving from the observation deck.
Move a hand back and forth as the jet leaves the gate,
taxis toward the runway. Everyone waits to be lifted.

(When I was a boy I almost drowned in the lake
called the Fifty-Footer. A man who saw me go down
put his hands under my arms, raised me to the yellow
light, and said, you can breathe now.)

Airborne, we level off at 33,000 feet, the earth below
a paradigm of green and hay colored squares. I close
my eyes to the sun, listen to the white noise in the cabin,
try to imagine the darkness we move toward, how time
changes. I awaken to a movie on multiple screens.
No sound but I've seen it before. This is the part
where a man says to a woman, I love you.
Under my breath I say I love you to the man
who saved me, to those I'm leaving behind.
They embrace without saying a word.

Sea Willow

I think of sand, how it reforms in the wind.
Think of wind, the formless. I have come back
to the windiest point in North America, to the light-
house and the lens floating in a drum
of quicksilver.

And recall the Japanese pilots of World War II,
flying Zeros, their vision so precise
they could locate stars in the day,
using locked points in the sky
as guides.

And I think of the sounds and shapes
when we weren't here. No fingers
for sand to slip through, no voices.
And what of after? After we're gone.
Old thoughts really. Today's noon
falters as I walk back to my car parked
between white lines. I turn to look
again at the bare sea willow, the empty
sand.

Lesson

Our lay teacher, Mr. G, taught us Bible history.
What is sweet to the mouth is bitter
to the stomach, he said. I never saw him at church.
He always ate a Milky Way bar during
study period. One of the deadly sins at St. Mary's.
He thought no one saw him take small bites
from the hidden candy in his pencil drawer.
He'd let the chocolate-covered caramel
and nougat melt, lick his lips after swallowing.
The crinkle of wrapper as loud as a cheat
sheet in the back of a freshman classroom.
We, who could hear the hum of a clock's
second hand behind glass, knew. I asked
him if the apple Adam ate was sweet
and did Eve help finish it or was it just two
bites. He said it was delicious.
And they took their pleasure, ate it all.
Next school year he was gone.

Instruction at Fifteen

We were lying face down on the ground, left foot
across the right, looking through our scopes.
I could feel the earth's press, could see everything.
You said, "Aim for the heart, not the head; don't wound
him; don't ruin the antlers." I could see everything.
There was not a single cloud. Some leaves waiting
for winter wind. He stood there, stock still. And I
squeezed, lifting the barrel slightly. It was enough;
the shot went wild. There were several moments
of quiet. The birds squawked, and I heard my uncle's
words as he rolled onto his side: "Forgot to tell you,
don't miss." No wind stirred. I could see everything,
the leaves, their drift to earth.

Evidence

They string the buck up
by his hind quarter. He
twitches one last time.
A quick slash near the scrotum
and blood flows in a slow stream
to the hungry soil. They chop
the hooves off, peel the hide
away, the head and antlers
prized, evidence of the good
hunt. A fire is built with green wood.
Smoked slowly, the meat cooks
to a sweet jerky. The men sit
on their haunches, smoking,
taking pulls from a 5th
of sour mash.
5000 years ago
Miwok hunters slew
a stag at this very spot and dressed
the animal where it fell. The tapered
horn was made into a necklace,
hide stretched over embers to dry,
the blood drunk from gourd bowls
heavy in their hands.
Time and form merge:
polished bone tossed to the earth.
Ghosts caught in the act.

The Armadillo

The ears are not quite right,
too much like a hare, but the body with overlays
of metal is perfect. And the eyes, cutouts
done with a welding torch, have a look
of both menace and passivity. The perimeter
of its armor is jagged, like the teeth of a ripsaw.
And ugly, useless as a paper weight
because it leaves dents, or as something to put
on a coffee table, because it detracts.
It was a gift I got on White Elephant Day,
the year it rained too much. I will pass it along
to friends in Albuquerque, because they're used to living
next to the monsters at Alamogordo and Los Alamos.
They'll probably chuck it or put it out
along the roadside with the plastic-flower memorials,
and the iron armadillo will rust, start to look real.
Passing motorists may slow down to see
if it moves, or shoot at the two big ears with a .22,
and the sun will wear down
the body, like those who have lost
someone and cannot forget.

Thinking

What were you thinking when you threw
your new pair of shoes out the window?
And though it was cold, dirty snow
on the ground, piles of it over the curb,
some cars stuck in ruts of ice, you took off
your clothes too, let them fly out, flapping
their way down three stories, like old
newspapers in the public park, blowing
around the bare elms and the once fiery
ailanthus, because it was winter, spring
not even around the corner, and then
your whole body, your whole life followed
through the dormer, and you came to your own
immortality, the shoes and the clothes,
the broken pieces; the police picking everything up,
packing them away like peaches, in those wooden
and wire crates they used to make for fruit
that could bruise easily, and you then turning
white from a powdery snow just starting,
and some of the neighbors stepped out
onto their porches and stoops, and some closed
their storm doors and shutters, and made
supper because it was that time of day,
because they were hungry, and could do nothing
to stop.

October 10th

The roofers unpeel the flashing,
tear up old tar and gravel, scrape away
three layers of sheathing, replace the plywood
on eighteen inch eaves. The whole house
shakes. Inside the walls: sounds of muffled
firecrackers. On the roof: lion dancers. I close
the windows, the doors, stay in the shudder
and listen to the thumps of hundred pound rolls
of tar paper, the shouts of men hauling
hods and hot mops. In two days, windrush
and leaf scatter, the trees fluting. Sky, chrome blue.
Nearby, dogs hoarse from barking, lie exhausted.
I spread my arms wide, like a tree in this new peace,
this degree of silence, and sing off key for rain
to come. I'm dancing now, lifting one knee,
then the other, stomping on the deck,
raising a racket.

Painting

Today I'm painting the eaves on my house
a color called Brushwood. Fifteen years ago
it had a different name, Truffle. And the spiders
and their webs I cleared away yesterday,
with a mix of bleach and water, are rebuilding,
a bittersweet effort to reconnect, to turn their lives
around. It is a perfect day to paint, mid-sixties,
fresh smells of early fall, the leaves holding out
new hues of sienna and yellow. The spiders drop
from their tenements on fine lifelines. I know
the moss will return to the overhang, then go
rusty-gold in summer, and the spiders will continue
the dispiriting task, tying nearly invisible knots
from flashing to downspout, every corner redefined.
I roll out more paint, feather edges with a brush,
try to change.

Visiting

This is how I remember him: leaning back in a kitchen chair,
eyes closed, alone among us. Arrogant. Indestructible,
unlike the family folded around him. I'm reminded
of the Hesse story about a man who wished for immortality
and became a mountain and sat century after century,
millennium to millennium. A god. Digger pines sticking
out of his belly, goats walking up his beards of gravel,
a glacial hat worn by a weatherman suspicious of the changing
seasons, past remembering what he had become. Forgetting
he was the mountain. Waiting. Alone. My father.
Dead except for the picture I've kept
of the kitchen chair.

Building the Ordinary

He built a wall from railroad ties pilfered from the Susquehanna,
their tracks and spikes long gone. He said, it wasn't stealing
if you put the unused to good use. And it was hard work lugging
those rough-milled logs soaked in creosote, digging footings
four feet deep, backfilling with stone, plain dirt. After it was done,
he sat propped against the wall, ate sun-warmed ripe tomatoes
and drank Knickerbocker beer from the bottle. He was close
to the earth, and I think it is holy when something is made
that can hold back time, last long after you're dead. It was a kind
of religion to him, and he cut in the year, 1954, with a chisel,
followed by A.D., in case some pope should change calendars,
and so no one would mistake this wall for something ordinary.

Two Bird Cafe

When I eat out, I want it to be outside,
if the weather's good, and the menu –
sometimes even if the weather and the wind are brisk
or summery, with the annoyance of yellow jackets
buzzing the plates of short ribs or Tony's Special –
scramble of spinach, onion, link sausage.
The Two Bird, the one in Forest Knolls, is gone,
as is the arbor covered in wisteria with green pods
drooping, and the waitress with a gap tooth,
who would always smile, God bless her,
and bring me seared rainbow trout, spuds,
country biscuits. I was never so happy, leaning back
in the white plastic chair looking into the vine
and back at the filleted trout, the mystery
of its body open, the white flesh, my hunger.

I think it was 1995 when they lost their lease,
closed and moved to another town closer in,
changed the oil cloth on the tables to linen,
the mismatched plates and flatware to conform.
I go there on and off. There's a year-round
creek running. Country style pork chops,
fancy omelets on the sandwich board,
and the prices are up, not that I remember
the old prices. It was too good then to care.

continued

I want it to be as it once was: want the wisteria,
want the waitress who, by the way, wore a bustier,
and beads in her long curly hair, smiled.
I live between two memories, one always changing.
And I still have two seed pods that were satiny,
now darkened, hard, and a paper placemat
I wrote on and took with me, because it was a first
draft, because it was better and could take off
in the wind, if I didn't hold.

How a Day is Spent

Marshall is a place, not Johnny Law, the long arm,
and it's east not west on Tomales Bay, which feeds
in and out from the Pacific. And there's a place there
I go to get oysters, family run, open Friday thru Sunday.
They take only cash and check. So you know the line
at the door starts at 11:30 am, the catch hauled
to the cleaning sinks and the kitchen around the same time.
I learned after going there on and off for nineteen years,
maybe closer to twenty, that the seeds
for the bivalves are shipped from Japan each season
because they need warmth to incubate; then they need
the constant flow of fresh and cold to grow. I always tip big
here and round up high, sometimes have an iced Anchor
Steam beer, maybe a mile walk out and back
to the full parking lot, maybe strike up a conversation,
because talk is a way to share. Because the days go
from short to long and back, I fast for the rest of the day,
as eating is a kind of religion without name.

Where Things Meet What is Taken

I'm out at Limantour Beach again, walking
due north this time, on the 31st of March,
the twenty-fifth day of rain, and alone.
Though moments before a horse galloped
past, saddleless, naked without rider.
And as I watched him move
far away, he became more.
Just as when the tide pulls back,
the shore broadens.

Each Thing Reminds

For me, a train whistle far off
says the Pine Barrens of New Jersey,
the smell of huckleberries ripening,
and humid summer nights,
the chorus of katydids, the silence
from one side of the woods waiting.
But some things are solid, well seated.
They live in a space of their own making,
outside memory's tampering.

I will tell you one.

The time I stumbled upon a dog
who had ripped open the throat
of a lamb. The look he gave me
as he gorged himself on the liver
and would not stop.

Living Fences

Who lives alone and is happy?
God comes to mind. So infinite, yet no one
can get close. His angels act as guards.
They keep creation distant.
And the fallen? Look where they are.
What can compare to loneliness?
Now, because it is April, month of rebirth,
birds clamor in the flowering purple quince
with longing. And old yellow dogs eye
their fences. They too feel longing,
and acceptance. They understand. Eden,
garden of limits, is no longer
where they are.

On the Way from One Place to Another

The motel had a swimming pool,
though no one would go near it
because of all the scum and floating filth.
And the room had a funny smell,
the TV only one station with a wavering
horizontal line from bottom to top and back.
But this was a road trip and it was cheap, only one night,
check out at 11a.m.
                    Who wants to remember
this stuff anyway? Except that I met someone
in the lobby, and we sipped scalded coffee,
talking about this and that, then ended up
drinking vodka from each other's belly button
in our rooms, where adjoining doors
made a suite out of a dump. Neither of us
liked the taste of vodka, or the burn,
but what else we did made up for it.
How is it memory can have no name
to go with a face or even a place?
                    A motel
off the highway, between two cities,
and the desk clerk gave us a smile, said something nice.
And now that I think back, didn't charge enough.

Afterword

We spend half our lives burying, half
tending. Careful to prune only after
the last chance of a cold snap. We save
and savor, and at the same time burn
what we want to lose. It is the circle of things.
These words owe their lives to paper,
invention of the paper wasp. Conjure the bite,
the pain. What follows: the beauty?

About the Author

Fairfax, California poet Joseph Zaccardi is Associate Editor of the Marin Poetry Center Anthology. He teaches *Transformations: a Poetry Tutorial*, and volunteers at the Rafael Convalescent Hospital reading to individual residents. His poems have appeared in Seattle Review, Runes, Southern Poetry Review, Baltimore Review and elsewhere. He received a grant from the Marin Arts Council in 2003 for his first book, *Vents*, which was published in 2005.

Printed in the United States
145138LV00003B/3/P